Holding It Together

Surviving a Legacy
of Mental Illness

A Memoir

Joan Kantor

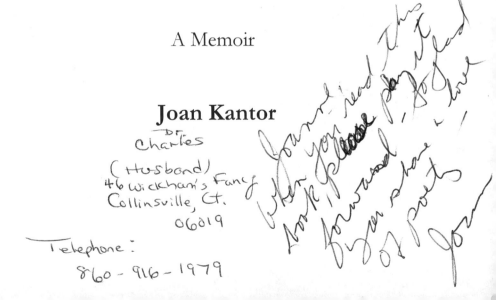

Dr.
Charles
(Husband)
46 Wickham's Fancy
Collinsville, Ct.
06019

Telephone:
860 - 916 - 1979

ISBN-13: 978-0692625859
ISBN-10: 0692625852
Library of Congress Control Number: 2016931706
WovenWord Press, Canton CT

Legacy *

I never knew my grandfather
He died
when I was only two

My mother told me
he kept to himself
and couldn't get along
with others

She never saw him kiss her mother
and though he didn't often smile
offer hugs
or hold his youngest child's hand
he'd buy her Cracker Jacks
and take her on long walks
to Fort Tryon Park

Mostly though
she remembers him
lost in sadness
threatening suicide
and vanishing for days

He waited till she was grown
to end his sadness
in The East River

never knowing
it would come alive
in me**

*My grandfather, after struggling with untreated depression for most of his life,
jumped to his death, in the East River, from the Brooklyn Bridge.
**My sister and cousins all have struggled with diagnoses of bipolar disorder.

Introduction

This book is quite different from others I have written, being that it is a hybrid of prose and poetry, though it is certainly more focused on poetry. The poems are meant to be easily read. They reflect my personal experience of mental illness, which has been of severe clinical depression, periods of severe anxiety, and mild hypomania. I am in no way trying to speak for others, whose experiences may be quite different from mine. The final poem in this book is the one exception; in it I am offering an alternate lens through which to look at those who suffer from the most severe forms of mental illness.

In this book I have broken with my usual writing style, in that I have not edited out or used synonyms for certain words that are repeated throughout the work. These words are powerful to me and truly express what I'm thinking during bouts of mental illness. The term "Grim Reaper" may seem corny, odd, or even melodramatic, but it is exactly what I think of each time I sense a bout of depression coming on.

I have a strong affinity for water and so you will often see words like *floating* and *sinking*. Other words that you'll frequently see are *sadness, shame, gut, mask, sinkhole, darkness* and one that is thematic to this work, *desperation*. Authenticity is always important in writing, but even more so when the topic is so serious and personal. I am baring my soul and I've chosen to do so with total honesty, even in my use of language.

The writing of this book was a painful but necessary journey. I have always felt that people need to hear from the mentally ill, in order to better understand what living both with and without the disease is like for us. The troubling randomness and intermittent nature of it creates a sense of frightening anticipation, almost as bad as the actual illness itself.

I want people to know that, for some of us, there is also a positive side to the suffering. We are often gifted with an abundance of creativity which can, at times, bring an extraordinarily powerful sense of joy and fulfillment.* Many of us, unlike most people, actively appreciate every moment of each day that we are alive and well. Some of us have also lost the fear of death. It's important to mention too that some of the most creative and productive people throughout history have struggled with mental illness during their lifetimes.** We have much to offer the world.

*I have often wondered if that gift is a mixed blessing. Perhaps such a generous gift is more than any body or mind is capable of handling. Along this line of thinking, many of us struggle with taking our meds for fear that they may rob us of our creativity.

** Sylvia Plath, Virginia Woolf, Ernest Hemingway, Cole Porter, Frida Kahlo, Georgia O'Keefe, Charles Mingus, Kurt Cobain, Edvard Munch, Franz Kafka, Ezra Pound, Robert Lowell, Charles Darwin, Eugene O'Neill, Friedrich Nietzsche, Ludwig van Beethoven, Jackson Pollock, Kurt Vonnegut, David Foster Wallace, Mark Rothko, Edgar Allen Poe, Hector Berlioz, Robert Schumann, Charles Parker, Tchaikovsky, Rachmaninoff, Carrie Fisher, Patty Duke, Brian Wilson, William Styron, Joan Miro, John Keats, Leo Tolstoy, Mike Wallace, Vaslav Nijinsky, Tennessee Williams, John Nash, Isaac Newton, Jim Carrey, Jane Pauley, Michelangelo, Charles Dickens, Winston Churchill, Theodore Roosevelt, Abraham Lincoln, Buzz Aldrin, Vincent Van Gogh and many, many more.

That Creative Connection

I recently went to a comprehensive chronological exhibit on Van Gogh's life and work. I'd had no idea how much he had struggled throughout his entire lifetime to get along with others, and that he'd been serially unsuccessful in his pursuits, including the ministry. I was unaware that he hadn't discovered art until his late twenties, and that his work was fairly pedestrian until the mid-1880s. He died in 1890 at the age of 37. Almost all of his best work was done during the last three years of his life. How tragic, yet magnificent, was the inner world that mental illness helped create in him and that will live on as a powerful artistic legacy. I've wondered what he was actually experiencing and trying to reproduce from within his mind. He clearly was seeing things differently than most people. The resulting brilliance was so great that despite my personal experience of mental illness, I long to gain access to his distorted, yet beautiful, visions and thought processes. The poem on the following page is an expression of that longing.

Through His Eyes

His work was mediocre
until the last years of his life
when the light-filled hues
of impressionism
and the linear structure
of Japanese prints
flipped an artistic switch
that took him further
than any artist had gone before

but there was more at play

Along with his brilliant undulating flowers
mental illness had fully bloomed

and as a part of him was dying
another came alive

full of texture
vibrant colors
and line

As his feverish soul
began to veer from the path
into a wilderness of madness*
he furiously worked
with his brushes and paints
creating skewed perspectives
dark contoured edges
solid saturated patches
vibrant otherworldly colors
and thick swirls of impasto strokes
in hundreds of paintings

as if he knew
his life
would soon be over

and though I don't long
for the darkness and pain
I want so much more
than a well-painted facsimile
on a museum wall

For one brief moment
I long
to see the world
exactly as he saw it
from inside

* *Though I am fully aware of this word's negative connotations, I have chosen to use it in the context of history.*

Dedications

This book is dedicated to the memories of my grandfather, Bernard "Barney" Newhoff, and Alex Kochkin. It is also dedicated to my dear friend Anna Kochkin, as well as all those who have either suffered the anguish of mental illness or have loved someone who has.

I want to especially and deeply thank my husband, Chuck, for without his steadfast devotion, sense of humor, creative thinking, and relentless determination, I would not have been here to share this work with others.

I want to thank my daughter, Leah, for being there for me throughout my illness. Even though she was just a child during much of it, she had a kind and nurturing touch. Her love, and my love for her, helped me more than she will ever know.

I also want to thank my wonderful friend and mentor, Rennie McQuilkin, from whom I have learned so much, as well as my friends Cheryl, Elaine, and June for listening to so many of my poems and giving wonderfully honest feedback.

Grace Epstein's powerful, though tiny, sculpture was always meant to be the cover image for this book. For years, I've kept it in a prominent place and it has consistently reminded me to appreciate every moment that I am alive and well. Thank you, Grace.

Table Of Contents

Living The Legacy / 1

Freedom

Equality / *10*
Reversal / *11*
Last One Out / *12*

The Enemy

Having It Out With Melancholy / *16*
Prodrome / *17*
On The Edge / *18*
Who's Boss / *19*
Bipolar Battle / *20*
Depression Lesson / *22*
Anxiety 1 / *24*
Anxiety 2 / *25*
Feeling His Pain / *26*
Desperation / *27*
At A Loss / *29*
At Its Whim / *30*
Once Again / *31*
Saving Self / *32*

Shockwaves

Shock / *36*
Aftershocks / *38*
Growth / *40*

Seeing The Light

Survival / *42*
Not This Time / *43*
Back To Life / *45*
Don't Look Back /*46*
Wouldn't Change A Thing /*47*
A Gift /*48*
Building Strength / *49*

Postscript /*51*

Fear Not / *53*

Living The Legacy

I'd always wondered why my grandfather had jumped from the Brooklyn Bridge. Though he had threatened suicide many times throughout his marriage, no one I asked seemed to know why. They described him as always being an unhappy and difficult man, but they came up empty when I asked for reasons.

Even during my childhood, though I never knew my grandfather, there were definite signs that his blood ran through my veins. I was difficult and painfully shy, bit my nails, whined and worried about everything. Fear engulfed me and I remember in fifth grade having months of sleepless nights over the teacher possibly seeing my sloppy handwriting. I was terrified of and had haunting thoughts about death. I was riddled with anxiety and often had a sinking feeling in the pit of my stomach, but I couldn't have known what these feelings meant. When I wasn't feeling down or anxious, I was bursting with joy and enthusiasm for life.

It wasn't until I was married and in my twenties that depression became a disruptive part of my existence. I had one particularly lengthy and extreme episode that was triggered by a sudden job loss. I sank into an abyss, which was frightening, not just for me, but for my husband as well. Afterwards, we both assumed that I had just had a difficult reaction to a bad situation, but I know now that circumstances had clearly triggered an underlying biochemical process.

I was in my late twenties when we started a family and was overjoyed with both pregnancy and new parenthood. When our first child was just a few months old, however, I once again sank into a deep depression that came on very suddenly. I fought it by regularly jogging and soon began to feel better. I believed I had just suffered from a relatively normal postpartum depression, but it came back and lasted longer with the birth of my second child. By the time my third and last child came along, no matter what I did, it wouldn't go away. Thus began my journey through the world of mental illness.

I saw several psychiatrists and tried numerous combinations of medication. Some of them worked for a while, but I always needed higher and higher doses, and this came with a price. For several years, I believed I had an undiagnosable variant of Lyme disease, since I suffered from daylong fatigue and painful joints. When I stopped taking the medication (which had become ineffective), I discovered that the meds had actually been the cause of all the symptoms. One drug I took even caused a three-week bout of totally incapacitating vertigo. Over and over again, the meds would stop working or I'd have terrible side effects. Early on, I would have long stretches of normalcy interspersed with episodes of depression. Eventually, that pattern would come to reverse itself. I learned to live one day at a time.

I gradually began to put the pieces together, realizing that the disease was somehow related to hormones and other chemicals in my body. There was a clear correlation between childbirth, nursing, migraines and depression. For an entire year after I had my third child, I had severe migraines that alternated with bouts of depression. It was a relief, in a sense, to finally see the problem as being a biochemical one; I wasn't crazy at all—I had a medical disorder.

I was becoming angry and resentful that my life was being stolen. There were two different versions of who I was, and I knew that the empty and depressed one was not the real me. The onset of depression is such a physical experience that I could almost feel the hand of what I came to call "The Grim

Reaper" tapping me on the shoulder; I can remember the gripping sense of dread that would come over me. No matter how wonderful my circumstances were, I just couldn't fend off the depression. I tried to squeeze a full life into the spaces between episodes of the illness. I was a pretty good actress too; most people wouldn't have been able to tell that I was losing control of my life. I was managing to deal with three ADHD/learning disabled children, one of whom was extremely challenging. I even went back to school for a master's degree, and though I would never be able to handle a full-time job, I found a wonderful part-time career as a counselor and disabilities specialist at a local community college. It was difficult having to hide the truth of my illness, but I had decided never to give up the fight and to live as fully as possible. Keeping this painful secret (with a few very special exceptions) was necessary, in order to achieve that.

Sadly though, several times during those difficult years, ending my life began to seem like a viable and totally logical choice. I love life, and would often struggle with the beautiful memories of what had once been a wonderful existence. But as that life began to seem impossibly far away, I came to see death as a welcome and peaceful escape from endless pain. I began to see that death could be a gift, and not something to be feared. Most people see depression as a purely mental state, but, at least for me, this is not the case. It's actually centered in the core of my body, in a giant sinkhole. It may be difficult for others to understand that sadness can be manifested in the body as well as the mind. It's much more about what I physically feel than what thoughts I may have; the suicidal ideation was simply a reaction to the former.

I thought often about not wanting to hurt my family. Like my grandfather who waited until his seven children were grown, I managed to hold suicide at bay while mine were young.

Every time I sank down deep, it seemed impossible that there could be further down for me to go. Each bout, however, was worse than the last. When all of the drugs had finally been tried and there was no place left to go, I made the frightening decision to try electric shock therapy (ECT). I had seen it horrifically depicted in the film *One Flew Over The Cuckoo's Nest* and was absolutely terrified, but my desperation overcame the fear. It turned out to be nothing like I expected; the staff were respectful and kind, and the experience was anything but barbaric.*

In spite of that, I would go in as a totally aware, though depressed, person, and come out as a zombie. I had no sense of time or place, and all memory had been zapped from my brain. Amazingly, however, I left with a huge smile on my face; the sinkhole had been filled, while the brain had been emptied. I couldn't even recall the name of my closest friend who had to drive me to and from the appointments (ECT is given not just once, but in a series). I wasn't permitted to drive at all in between the treatments, and I would go home and sleep the debilitating side effects off while waiting for brain function to return. It took weeks to months for most of my memories to come back; short-term memory was permanently and embarrassingly affected (I had always had an excellent memory) and I still have odd little gaps in my long-term memory. Relief overcame frustration, and I came to feel like a happily demented elderly person, but it was very difficult for my husband and family to see me that way.

The first ECT experience was very successful. It gave me back my life for almost an entire year. The effects of the second series of ECT only lasted a few months. It's possible to have maintenance ECT (monthly), but I knew that I would forever be different from the person I wanted to be. I truly felt that there was no hope. My children were grown, and this time suicide became a real option.

The procedure is quite different than it once was. The patient is unconscious, under anesthesia, and there are mild twitches rather than the oft-described flailing body parts.

The following is a brief explanation of how we finally found an effective treatment. Though it may be a bit dense, I think you will find it well worth wading through. My husband, a physician, always has been one to think outside of the box. Feeling my desperation, he began to explore every possible option. Since I was already taking a fairly high dose of an SSRI*, he was concerned about adding other chemicals that might raise my serotonin levels (brain serotonin is one of the primary chemicals that regulates mood), potentially causing what is known as The Serotonin Syndrome.** He decided to get my blood tested for levels of serum serotonin (no doctors had ever suggested this before). Remarkably, when my blood test results came back, they showed that I had virtually no detectable levels. He then began to consider whether serum serotonin and brain serotonin might be related (this relationship is not yet understood). In an attempt to raise my serum serotonin levels I began taking tryptophan, which the body converts to 5-hydroxytryptophan(5HTP), and later to serotonin. Despite increasing doses, my levels of serum serotonin never increased. I then started taking 5HTP. We had to experiment with the dosage of 5HTP, since, unfortunately, there are currently no established guidelines on how to use it for a mood disorder*** and there can be serious side effects (monitoring by a physician is of the utmost importance).

*SSRI stands for selective serotonin reuptake inhibitor, one of the major classes of drugs used in the treatment of depression.

**The Serotonin Syndrome can manifest as agitation, confusion, rapid heart rate, sweating, muscle rigidity, diarrhea and headache. When severe, it can cause high fever, seizures, abnormal heart beats and unconsciousness.

***There have been no large scale clinical studies on 5HTP and its relationship with brain serotonin levels.

Finally, my serum serotonin levels began to improve. I don't believe in miracles, but the very next day I had a sense of well-being and balance. This has been the case for over five years, with only one brief loss-related bout of depression. I still need to take a low dose of an SSRI antidepressant along with the 5HTP, and I know that depression might still return someday, but for now and into the foreseeable future, I am free from this devastating illness. Like everyone, I now have normal ups and downs that are related to life circumstances. They are probably higher and lower than most people's but that is what makes me who I am. I was able to publish a book of poetry (*Shadow Sounds*, Antrim House 2010) and I have been doing readings as well as performances with a professional violinist. I am fully enjoying my family, as well as my friends and work. Though I have written poetry my entire life, my creativity has been unleashed and it is virtually pouring onto the page these days. I recently published my second collection, *Fading Into Focus* (about Alzheimer's Disease and a mother-daughter relationship), and it took First Place for Poetry in The 2015 *Writer's Digest* Self-Published Book Awards Contest.

There are heroes in this story. My grandfather somehow managed to find the courage to support a family of nine while suffering so deeply. My husband never gave up on me, no matter how difficult life became. He took on whatever needed to be done so that the family could function. Ultimately, he even saved my life. I no longer have to wonder why, on that fateful day, over sixty years ago, my grandfather probably looked down longingly at the East River from The Brooklyn Bridge. Had he lived today, it's possible that he may never have had to jump; he may have just needed to take an anti-depressant and/or up his level of serum serotonin with 5HTP or some alternative.

Had I known what I now know, perhaps I would have been able to avoid those damaging two courses of ECT. In spite of this, I'm still pleased with where I am today and have made the choice not to dwell in the past. I have always believed that there is something to be gained from every experience. Depression has given me a unique and wonderful perspective. It has enriched my writing, my work, my relationships and appreciation of just about everything. I no longer have a fear of death and every moment is that much more precious; I worry very little these days. I only hope that there will be more research into 5HTP (as well as Ketamine* and other alternative treatments) and the serum serotonin/brain serotonin connection.. I hope that others, suffering as I have, will someday also be given the possibility of once again experiencing a full and joyful life.** Many people who suffer from depression respond to the traditional therapies, but for those of us who do not, it is so important to have alternatives. There are probably other options that I'm unaware of; all of them need to have their efficacy proven through proper clinical research in order for physicians to feel comfortable recommending them. The motivating force behind research should be saving lives and not profit.

This has not been the case with 5HTP, which is reasonably priced and readily available without prescription. Since there would be no profit in researching the benefits of 5HTP, big pharmaceutical companies have little incentive in researching it. My plan is to contact government agencies and mental health institutions that might have some

*Ketamine is a widely used anesthetic that has been shown, in infusion form, to dramatically diminish symptoms of suicidal depression. So far, unfortunately, it has not received FDA approval, as its safety profile has not yet been established.

**5HTP is certainly not the answer for all who suffer from depression. Not everyone with the illness has very low serum serotonin levels and blood tests are necessary to determine if that is the case. Though 5HTP is available over the counter, unfortunately as an unregulated supplement, it should only be taken under the supervision of a licensed physician.

influence and/or money to help get these studies going.   It's a mission for me. I'm one of the lucky ones, but health should never have to be about luck.

Though I have been selectively open about my bipolar 2* diagnosis, I have chosen to formally "come out" with this book in order to share, with a wider audience, my experiences and viewpoint on mental illness as primarily a biochemical disease that is often genetically based.**

I hope the descriptions of depression and anxiety in this book will be helpful to loved ones who want and/or need to have a better understanding of what their family members or friends are going through. I also hope that they will make those who are suffering feel less alone.

My greatest hope for this book, other than encouraging more research about alternative therapies, is that it will open the eyes of those who judge and fear us. The disease, in its many forms, is extremely painful, and we should not have to also suffer from shame. Mental illness is the only "difference" still left in the closet, and it's about time that it be set free!

*Bipolar 2 is a mixed mood disorder that involves episodes of depression and hypomania (a mild form of mania). It is primarily a disorder of depression.

** It can also be triggered by external events

Freedom

*We sometimes forget that the brain is really just another organ in the body and when it doesn't work right, disease is the result. Cancer, Parkinson's, depression, schizophrenia, Alzheimer's, Creutzfeld-Jakob's, and bipolar disorder are **all** diseases of the brain.*

Equality

A powerhouse
of magnificent perfection
the boss
of the body
sometimes goes awry
and we who suffer
share a mixed desperation
of loss and hope
in the side effects and possible cures
that might come from our meds
but only some of us
have to swallow
a dose of shame
then hide
behind a mask
of feeling fine

It's a terrible feeling, wanting to be authentic yet needing to be selective in who you tell about a mental illness. There is such a stigma attached to it and the fear of misperception and judgment is powerful.

Reversal

I sometimes identify
with mimes
dressed head to toe
in black
silent
their white-gloved hands
pressing invisible walls

but they exude
a sense
of jovial desperation

My invisible walls
are much too real
my jagged desperation
painfully stifled

There's no joy
for me
in hiding the truth

Last One Out

I cautiously peek from the closet
desperate to share
my most recent release
from despair

It's so quiet
so lonely
still hiding inside

and just like those
who've already left
I long to be seen

to celebrate self
and survival

and to share
how pain brings perspective
creativity
and the intense rapture
of intermittent joy
that few
can ever hope
to understand

I never had a choice
but wouldn't change my fate
though others fearing it
pretend I don't exist

Genes and bio-chemicals
are the clay
from which we all build our lives

Though mine may be different
it has worth
not shame

and so I've decided
to push the door open

Watch Out World

Ready or Not

HERE I COME

The Enemy

The title of this poem was a writing prompt in a Poetry Therapy training session.

Having It Out With Melancholy

Melancholy
such a lovely lilting word
but you don't fool me

Too many times
I've sounded you out
Trying to use reason
I've rolled your dirge
around on my tongue
and in my heart

then too late
tried to spit you out
before I drowned

There's nothing that's gentle
or kind about you
in your cloak
of black armor
Darth Vader
Grim Reaper
with weapons well hidden

Keep your distance

Don't tap me
on the shoulder
with that long gnarly finger
for as soon
as you do
I'll be undone

Though I have had this experience numerous times, it is just as common for me to have no preparation for a sudden bout of depression.

Prodrome

Though in denial
I know
I'm feeling too good
which always means
I'm losing control
that pain and joy
are beginning to merge
in a vibrating aura of brightness
but frightened
I'd rather pretend I'm in charge
of this racing body and mind
and not flying so high
that I'll hit the ceiling
and suddenly slide
into darkness

On The Edge

My belly sinkhole
sucks life through
stealing hunger pangs

What's left
is a vague remembrance of joy
turned inside-out
wrung dry

Isolation mocks me

It peels off my mask
and settles its hollow ache
in my gut

My body recoils
from the jagged edges
of sleep

Loved ones reach out soothingly
and teetering
on the edge
I stretch

to barely feel
their touch

Who's Boss

He's never far behind
and though I pretend
it isn't so
I know he's always stalking
just waiting
for a moment of weakness
or a cocky false sense of safety
an extended period
of inner peace
or joy
when for what seems to be
no reason at all
he taps me on the shoulder
and unsuspecting
I turn around
to meet his piercing gaze
as he suddenly grips my head
in his hands
with unbearable pressure
then stabs me
in the gut
ripping through layers of meds
and filling my body and soul
with a sinking sadness
leaving me lifeless
as he absconds
with all hope

This poem was inspired by one of Simsbury artist Ruth Jacobson's paintings. I identified with the spirit of the woman in the picture, though clearly we look nothing alike. I decided to use her physical image, instead of mine, in the poem.

Bipolar Battle

Passionate
fun
a little loopy
and over the top
she celebrates
her bold orange hair
while wrapped
in billowing brilliant red
that only she can wear

Yet being so colorful
makes the contrast
with imminent darkness
too clear
and trying to hide the fear
almost too much to bear

For her
there's no in-between

but she won't give up hope

and so this time
        as her heart begins to race
and unnatural brightness
            dominates

        knowing the edge
     is straight ahead
and that soon
       she'll fall

she takes
a slow
deep
deliberate
breath

closes her eyes
till she finds
the distant pastel pool
of her innermost calm
and meditates
to will herself
afloat

While suffering from depression, I always knew that my illness had a major impact on family members. I made it a point to hold it together as much as I possibly could, but there were times where my attempts to do so were futile.

Depression Lesson

dedicated to my daughter Leah

My little girls sits
at the edge of my bed
with love and concern
in her eyes
as I try to look happy
but no longer can

and I watch us switch roles
as she gently strokes my arm
and tries to convince me to eat

She leaves my side
and quickly returns
with a chocolate shake
and tentative smile

Guilt infiltrates
the depths of my sadness

She's taken on a burden
that's impossibly large

What will happen
if she someday believes
that she failed me

I'm not sure what she knows
so I try to explain
between tiny labored sips
but it's impossible

How can *she* understand
what *I* can't

I've chosen to share more than one poem about depression, mania and anxiety, because mental illness is very slippery and changes its persona often. Each time you think you understand the symptoms, prodrome, or triggers, it has a sneaky habit of changing and throwing you off.

Anxiety I

I'm a live wire
    felled by an inner storm
        body abuzz
with vibrating
    tingling skin
short-circuiting

a twitching
    writhing
        wriggling snake
flung up
    and down
        smacking the ground
hissing
    bright orange sparks
in the darkness

Anxiety II

Gripping my guts
    you rumble
        my roots
    and in waves
        rising up
           and spreading out
              you shiver my skin
    in an endless
   low magnitude earthquake
  that rattles and roars
pushes and pulls
    yet never breaks
        the surface

I decided to share this poem about Vincent Van Gogh, because when I looked at it, I felt a powerful kinship. The anxiety, that I know so well, virtually jumped from the painting. He painted this self-portrait in 1887, three years before taking his own life.

Feeling His Pain

Who did he think
he was fooling
when he sat so still
and painted himself
with that sober mask
of clenched control
when his brush-strokes
were streaks of electric sparks
rushing from his eyes
overtaking his face
till every vibrating hair
on his head
was standing on end

The following two poems were written after I experienced a particularly terrible drug reaction. There were no more antidepressants left for me to try, and so the psychiatrist experimented with an anti-psychotic, which worked in reverse. I got a brief window into the extreme confusion and suffering of those who deal with the most severe forms of mental illness.

Desperation

You're so tired of hearing
it's not a perfect science
but since there's nothing else left
you'll pop any pills
with little chance
of success

no matter the tremors
anxiety
mental fogginess
fatigue

till you lose your mind

You know the difference
between being depressed
and being out of touch
You're seeing things
that aren't there
and though you're trying hard
to speak
nonsense words
pour from your mouth
You've never been delusional
till now

You're missing your self
so much
but you're further away
than ever
and the world's become a blur
fading into the distance
You're trapped inside
behind thick metal walls
that no one else can see or feel
and though they desperately
want to help
they don't know how

You stop hoping
believing
trusting
longing
for anything but sleep

a living death
that offers
sweet relief

At a Loss

Dazed
Drifting
Dizzy
Drowsy

Outside
Inside
Inside-out

Weaving
Wobbling
Toppling

Sodden
Sinking

Surfacing suddenly
Somewhere
Wondering why
My body and mind
Won't let me find
Where I am

As I've mentioned before, mental illness is a real trickster. Every time you think you know what to expect, it throws you a curve.

At Its Whim

It usually happens
completely and quickly
but this time
is different

I've been able to stay
barely afloat
as it teases me
with the briefest
uplifting moments
of feeling fine
while its actually
slowly
pulling me down

and I don't know
why
when
or if

it will let me rise
or I'll finally drown

Once Again

Every night
I hope
I'll awaken
to health

and in the squinty eyed
newness of morning
I truly believe
I'm finally well

Then moments later
I realize I'm wrong

I try to will hunger
and happiness
but the fakery miserably fails

Fast fading
I drag myself
once again
through the darkness
of day

For me, the randomness of depression's onset is baffling. It often seems to have nothing to do with life's circumstances at all, although, at times, they can be a trigger or worsen an ongoing episode. Sadly, the inverse has never been the case for me.

Saving Self

I'm the happiest person alive
till someone
or something
or nothing at all
flips the switch
of the delicate balance
in my brain
where chemicals lurk
just lying in wait
to suddenly pounce
dig in their claws
drag me down
and once latched on
almost never let go
but still
I'll try
to will them away
with endorphins
and struggle
to slowly stand up
walk
run
swim
work out

then desperate
helpless
medicate
and with the little
I've left
meditate
to the mantra-memory
of my self

Shockwaves

Electric shock therapy was like nothing I could ever have imagined. The experience itself was so much gentler than I expected, but the after-effects were extremely challenging to live with.

Shock

You're desperate

Everything's been tried

The heaviness
weighs you down

You choose to relinquish yourself
to what used to be called barbaric

Your best friend drives you there

You sit down

The tv drones

They call your name

Familiar smiles greet you

Soon their faces
will loom
from above

You long
for what you don't want
but need

The anesthesia drip begins

The passage of time
disappears

You awaken
to a different world

once heavy
now weightless

once clear
now fog

and in the confusion
you wear a dopey smile

Someone you don't recognize
guides you by the hand

takes you home

where for weeks
you lie low

empty
with hope

Despite being told that the side effects of ECT would be temporary, some have never completely gone away. However, when you have experienced such severe clinical depression as I have, quality of life takes on a new meaning,

Aftershocks

My joy
allows me to work around
the long and short term memories
that are missing

Before the treatment
my mind took photos
that lasted forever

Now sometimes
they're fuzzy or blank

and I've learned
to preface all that I say
with " If I told you this before …"

I can dredge up arcane detailed facts
from the distant past
Then suddenly there are gaps

stories I can't recall

There's no clear pattern
just random holes
that I try to ignore
while trying to stop grieving
my loss

I remind myself
that I made a good choice
Losing fear
was worth losing pieces
that I don't even need
to be whole

Though I came to accept my limitations and redefined the meaning of wholeness and quality of life, this was not so easy a task for my family members.

Growth

Though my brain's been zapped
I can finally move forward with life
and once again fully experience joy

but my daughter says
I'm not who I was

Besides my no longer wanting to be

isn't that true
of us all

Seeing The Light

The will to live can be so powerful even when you're struggling with debilitating depression. There are memories of how beautiful life was and hope that the beauty will return. Just when you think you can't take it anymore, there is often a spark of life that pushes you forward toward survival.

Survival

Beneath heavy lids
my eyes sink deep
into the hollows
of their sockets

My arms and legs
are motionless logs

My heart's a throbbing rock
slowly falling
into a cavernous hole
between belly and chest

I'm so tired of trying to survive

Foggy and weak
I'm just begging for sleep

but tomorrow
I'll be back in the fight

This was one of those surprise poems. I thought I was writing purely about nature (I live on a river and frequently watch the fly fisherman fishing), but it turned out to be a metaphor.

Not This Time

I've broken free before
but there's leftover lead
in my belly

My heart and head are heavy
and the sharp metal hook
is digging in deep

Though weak
with pain
I wriggle and rush
through the rapids

Biting down hard
I whip my jaw
back and forth
as I drag the line
to the bottom
and slice it in half
with a snap
of sudden release

then hover
in disbelief

till slowly
in the darkness
I begin to swim free

Pretending the sinkers
are gone from my gut
gathering strength
I propel myself
and soar splashing
through the surface
with a flash of rainbow scales

then I eyeball the fisherman
flip him my tail
and spit the damn hook out

A small ceramic sculpture by Simsbury, Connecticut artist Grace Epstein, was the inspiration for this poem. It brings up so many emotions when I see it, and one of those is the sense of oversized joy I feel every time I escape from the shackles of depression. I chose this sculpture for the cover image, where it represents self-love, joy and pain.

Back To Life

Her mouth
is stretched
beyond open

lips pulled tightly back
teeth
palette
tongue
exposed

as she shrieks
with her entire being

From the tips
of her toes
to the top
of her head
every hair
is standing
on end

as lovingly she hugs herself
presses her hands
tight to her chest

and overflows
with the joy
of being back

At times, I have let the past paralyze me. Fear of the illness returning can too easily get in the way of enjoying the present and moving forward. I've had to consciously choose to ignore it. Even so, a dark image, of what I call "The Grim Reaper," tapping me once again on the shoulder, sometimes invades my consciousness.

Don't Look Back

I woke up this morning
finally able to part the fog
and with fingers tingling alive
found my way back
to my self

No more off-balance panic
of wondering where I was
or who I might possibly become

and as I jumped out of bed
onto solid ground
though a flutter of fear
almost made me turn around
I looked straight ahead
and placed one foot
in front of the other

This poem came about as the result of a poetry prompt, once again, during one of my Poetry Therapy training sessions.

Wouldn't Change A Thing …

… because I know what to do
with happiness

I dive right in
then slowly rise to the top

While soaking it in
I let go of petty problems
and a thrilling peacefulness
takes their place

Though it's always evanescent
happiness
when fearlessly savored
seems to last longer

As a sinking stone
I once hit bottom
but was lifted up
to finally see the meaning of joy
sniff out its subtle permutations
and though never to expect it
believe in possibilities
and cherish every moment
free of pain

A Gift

I used to be so afraid
of the end

until depression
gnawed a hollow
in my soul

and the gentlest hand
reached out
with the gift
of death

I saw peace
and beauty
in the offering

and knowing
it would always be there

I chose to live

This poem was inspired by an image of a Japanese bowl whose cracks were carefully filled in with what appeared to be solid gold. It is an example of **Kintsugi,** *the Japanese art of embracing damage. I'm not sure that these repaired ceramic pieces are literally stronger, but to many, there is beauty in both the breaking and the transformative repairs/ scars; a beauty that to me equals strength.*

Building Strength

Fingers of molten hot pain
insinuate themselves
into fissures
of a fragile soul
whose suffering
slowly hardens
into sturdy scars
that hold it together
stronger than ever

Postscript

I chose to include one additional poem that relates to individuals who deal with the most severe forms of mental illness. I believe that this particular population has suffered even more than the rest of us, especially from a sense of stigma. Until recently, there was no parity in the health care system for psychiatry and other mental health services. Often, individuals, unless they had excellent financial resources, were forced to go without diagnosis and/or treatment. It was not uncommon for people to self-medicate as a result (of course, stigma could have been and may still be a factor). A secondary drug addiction and the resulting problems often followed. Hopefully, with the new parity laws, this will be the case much less frequently.

The following poem relates to someone who, although her family has been able to afford treatment, still struggles from others' perceptions of the disease. I imagine that both she and her family would feel the need to avoid sharing her diagnosis with others.

Fear Not*

Pretty
petite
full of style
potential
and excited to launch
she was felled
on the cusp of college
by sneaky voices
telling her lies
and to be frightened
of life

While her friends
moved on
she lived with her folks
growing foggy
and overweight
from psychotropic drugs

and as if that weren't enough
the world's become paranoid
about people like her

Scapegoating the mentally ill
is easier than dealing with evil

Yet this plump young woman
with her still pretty face
is that same sweet girl
just battling inside
beneath the trappings of disease
while longing more than anything
to launch

Many researchers have found that people who have mental health issues are actually far more likely to be the victims of violence than to be the causes of it. The American Journal of Public Health found earlier this year that less than 5 percent of the country's 120,000 deaths related to gun violence between 2001 and 2010 were perpetrated by mentally ill people.

Also, according to the Journal, people diagnosed with schizophrenia, a severe psychiatric disorder, are 65 to 130 percent more likely to be victims of a crime than to commit one themselves.

Resource List

NAMI
National Alliance on Mental Illness
www.nami.org/

National Institute of Mental Illness
www.nimh.nih.gov/health/find-help/

Mental Health America
www.mentalhealthamerica.net/finding-help

American Psychiatric Association
www.psychiatry.org/

Substance Abuse and Mental Health Services Administration
www.samsha.org/

Ketamine Advocacy Network
www.ketamineadvocacynetwork.org/

University of Maryland
http://umm.edu/health/medical/altmed/supplement/5hydroxytryptophan-5htp

ABOUT THE AUTHOR

Award-winning poet Joan Kantor lives with her husband in the village of Collinsville, Connecticut. Joan's training is in education as well as marriage and family therapy, and she was a college counselor and disabilities specialist for many years. She actively promotes poetry in the community and is a member of the International Academy for Poetry Therapy. She has been a featured reader for the public television series *Speaking of Poetry* as well as for several art museums and galleries, and she has also been a featured poet in *The Avocet Literary Journal*. Additionally, she leads workshops, has mentored for Poetry Out Loud, and has judged and mentored for the Hill-Stead Museum's Sunken Garden Poetry Festival Fresh Voices Poetry Program. To fulfill her inclusive vision of the arts, Joan collaborates with both visual artists and musicians and currently performs in *Stringing Words Together*, an interactive performance of poetry and violin music.

Kantor's work has been widely published in literary journals and her first collection, *Shadow Sounds* (Antrim House 2010), was a finalist in the *Foreword Reviews* Book of the Year Awards Contest (2010). She won First Prize for Poetry in The 2013 Hackney Literary Awards Poetry Contest and in 2015 her book, *Fading Into Focus*, took First Place for Poetry in The 23rd Annual *Writer's Digest* Self-Published Book Awards Contest. Her next collection, *Too Close For Comfort*, will be published by Aldrich Press in 2016.

30618322R00047

Made in the USA
Middletown, DE
31 March 2016